big&SMALL

Original Korean text by Yun-hui Hong
Illustrations by Soon-ho Kim
Korean edition © Aram Publishing

This English edition published by big & SMALL in 2017
by arrangement with Aram Publishing
English text edited by Joy Cowley
English edition © big & SMALL 2017

Distributed in the United States and Canada by
Lerner Publishing Group, Inc.
241 First Avenue North
Minneapolis, MN 55401 U.S.A.
www.lernerbooks.com

ISBN: 978-1-925235-40-1
Printed in Korea

The Great Powers of Nature

Written by Yun-hui Hong
Illustrated by Soon-ho Kim
Edited by Joy Cowley

Nature is all around you. It's the animals, land, water, air, and more. Plants grow and animals and insects live in our natural world.

We also live in the natural world. We see that nature can be calm, but it can also be wild.

All living things need water.
Animals drink water.
Plants absorb water.

But sometimes it doesn't rain for a long time . . .

... and there's a **drought!**

Rivers dry up. The ground cracks.
Plants start to die and animals have
no food to eat.

Droughts happen over long periods of time.
They can last weeks, months, or years.

When it rains, everything starts growing again. Trees and plants turn green and the river fills with water.

But when there is too much rain…

. . . it can **flood!**

Water floods houses.
Dirt slides down hills.
The river overflows,
sweeping things away.

It takes hours or days for most floods to happen.
Flash floods happen very quickly.

The earth is made of rock
and dirt. We build houses,
roads, and buildings
on this hard ground.

But when the ground
suddenly shakes…

Earth's top layer is made of pieces. They are called plates. The plates move and sometimes they slip. This causes an earthquake.

. . . there's an **earthquake!**

The ground moves.
Buildings fall down.
They can bury people and hurt them.

Some mountains are volcanoes.
They have holes that go deep down
into the hot Earth. Heat from magma
warms water to make hot springs.

But if magma rises in the volcano . . .

Magma is melted rock under Earth's surface.
It is burning hot.

...it **erupts!**

The magma becomes lava
as it spills down from the volcano.
Lava flows over the land.
Ash covers the town.
Strong volcanic gases
make it hard to breathe.

Wind is moving air.
It dries our laundry
and cools our bodies.

But when the wind blows fast and strong . . .

. . . it's a **hurricane!**

Glass breaks! Walls collapse!
Power lines fall down
and roofs fly away!
A hurricane brings heavy rain
and can cause lots of damage.

A hurricane forms over warm ocean water. Its winds move in a giant swirl. At the center is the hurricane's eye.

Natural disasters happen, but we can
watch for their signs.
It can help us stay safe in nature.

We must look after nature
and not destroy it.
Our planet is our only home.

We can do things to stay safe in nature.
- Plant trees to reduce damage from droughts and floods.
- Monitor earth movement in places where there are
  earthquakes and live volcanoes.
- Build seawalls on beaches to protect the land from big waves.

Natural Disasters in the World

Each year, natural disasters occur in the world. Here are some of the largest natural disasters that have occurred.

Mount Vesuvius Eruption

Pompeii was a beautiful city in Italy at the base of the volcano Mount Vesuvius. In 79 CE, Mount Vesuvius erupted. Lava and ash completely covered the town, killing most of its population.

Haiti Earthquake

On January 12, 2010, a large earthquake hit Haiti. After the first shock, several smaller earthquakes occurred. Most buildings collapsed and buried people under them. Many people died or were injured.

Hurricane Katrina in US

In August 2005, the southern east coast of the United States was hit by Hurricane Katrina. More than 1,800 people died and millions of people were left homeless by the destructive wind and flooding after the hurricane.

East African Droughts

African countries such as Somalia, Kenya, and Ethiopia suffer from severe droughts. The hot sun blazes without relief from rain. It makes plants die and animals starve. As the drought worsens, people suffer from hunger and disease.

How Do Earth's Layers Affect Fault Lines?

Earth is made up of many layers. Each layer is called a stratum. More than one layer are called strata. Two of Earth's plates meet at a fault line. When the plates push against each other, they can make strata fold. When strata pushes up, it makes mountains grow. The bent strata also put pressure on fault lines, which can cause an earthquake. You can experiment with bending strata using modeling clay.

What you need:

Various colors of modeling clay

two clear acrylic boards

Instructions:

1

Make strata. Layer five different colors of modeling clay.

2

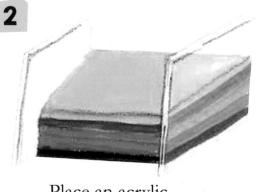

Place an acrylic board on either side.

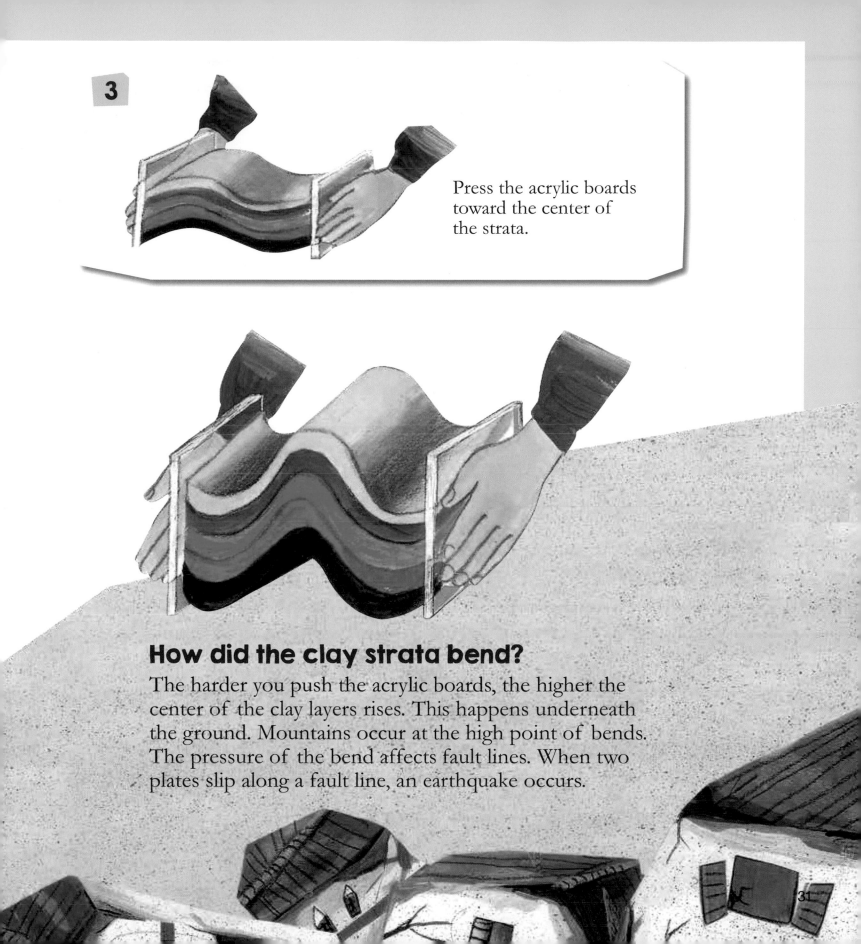

3

Press the acrylic boards toward the center of the strata.

How did the clay strata bend?

The harder you push the acrylic boards, the higher the center of the clay layers rises. This happens underneath the ground. Mountains occur at the high point of bends. The pressure of the bend affects fault lines. When two plates slip along a fault line, an earthquake occurs.

The Great Powers of Nature

Nature is all around us. Sometimes it shows its great powers. Floods happen after too much rain. Droughts dry the land. Volcanoes erupt, sending lava and ash into the air. Earthquakes shake buildings. And hurricanes bring heavy winds and rain.

Let's think!

What happens to the ground in a drought?

How can too much rain cause damage?

What causes an earthquake?

What is magma?

Let's do!

Make a hurricane! Put warm water in a bowl. Stir it in one direction for 15 seconds. Then drop some food coloring in the middle of the water. What shape does the color make? Do you see the "eye" of the hurricane? How does the spiral change over time?